What's up everyone, I want to talk about income streams, specifically the different income streams that exist in my business and technically kind of in my personal life that I make online. And so when I was browsing through Pinterest, I saw two graphics that really caught my eye. The first one is this graphic right here. And it basically outlines the eight different income streams that exist. Now if you're not familiar with the eight different income streams, let's just take a moment pull it up together, and go over it because I think it's really, really interesting and it's super enlightening to just expand your knowledge on the different types of income streams that exist in the world. So the first one is earned income.

This is income that we're all really familiar with, it's the income that you have to work for. So you have to actually earn it to make it. The second one is profit income at profit income is when you buy and sell things, and then that profit that you make from it, that's the income that you receive there.

So if I buy the shirt for 20 bucks, and then I sell it tomorrow for 40 bucks, then I've profited 20 bucks, interest income, this is the type of income that a lot of banks make. So if you lend money out, and then you charge interest on that, that is income that you make from that there is residual income. This is the income where you continue to get paid even after the work is done. So you do something once and then you get paid for it time and time after again, dividend income. This is the income that you make when you invest in stocks, and you get paid dividends from that rental income. This is income that we're also really familiar with. It's when you buy property, you rent it out and the income that you make from renting out that property that is your income there. There's capital gains. This is when an asset that you bought increases in value. So let's say you buy a house for a million dollars today. And then tomorrow, it's $2 million. That is capital gain. Another one that I'm not sure if it actually is capital gain, because I'm not sure if these are assets.

But let's say you buy a Birkin bag for $10,000 today and tomorrow with $20,000, that's also capital gain potentially. And then finally, there's royalty income. So a lot of singer songwriters make royalties. So this is when you sell your content, you sell your ideas, and then you make a kickback from that. And so when I was going through this list of eight income streams, it really got me thinking of how many income streams that I have.

Not only this, I also saw this graphic right here. And this graphic basically says that the average millionaire has seven income streams. And so I was like, Huh, I wonder how many I have. And so I started counting. And I started to actually look into the numbers. And as I was looking into the numbers, I was pretty impressed by some of the information that I found and I also didn't realize that I actually technically have six different types of income streams that I make online. So that's why I wanted to create this book because I thought it was really informative. And obviously this book is not meant for me to give you guys financial advice, but it is meant to be somewhat educational innocence where each income stream that I mentioned that I have, I'm going to try my best to kind of give you guys a quick tip for each one so that you're getting value out of it and you have action steps to take.

But also I hope that this book serves as inspiration of what is possible, because I see a lot of people stopping themselves from starting that YouTube channel, from starting that podcast show, from putting themselves out there, from building a personal brand. And it really really stinks to see that because for me before I started this YouTube channel, I started with two income streams: earned income and dividend income.

So to earn income whether it was me working at my corporate job or me working as a coffee barista, I had to work really hard to make money. The second income stream that I had was dividend income. So at the time I still have this income stream, I would invest in stocks, whether that was crypto currencies or index funds or stock picking, you know, I would make money off of that. And so at the time, I had two different types of income streams. But fast forward a year and a half later, almost two years later, since starting my channel, I now have six different types of income streams. A lot of it is thanks to me building and taking time to create this personal brand that I have online and building an audience that I have online. So long as you decide and you take that first step and that first leap of faith to create what you want to create online. There are so many awesome things that can happen as a ripple effect of you starting that channel, starting that podcast episode, starting that Instagram account and I really hope that this book serves as inspiration for that. Now, if you are interested in learning about the different income streams that I have the money that I make for each one, and also some actionable tips for you for each income stream, then this book is going to be perfect for you.

All right So let's dive into the first income stream that I have for you. And it's first for a reason because this income stream represents 80, if anything 90% of my monthly income, and that is selling digital courses. Now what this basically means is that I have package my knowledge on a particular subject. And in my case, my subject is all about helping new coaches create really great coaching programs, teach them how to sell and teach them how to use Instagram so that they can turn their followers into clients.

So what I've done is I've packaged all my knowledge surrounding this topic, and I've turned it into a digital course that can be accessible to anyone who has an internet connection. And by doing this, it has allowed me to create passive income streams for myself, because when you create digital products, an awesome awesome thing is that you only really need to do it once unless you're updating the course but to keep things simple, you really only have to do it once and what I mean by this is that You'll film the videos, filmed the tutorials, create the worksheets, do whatever you need to do to make it a really awesome experience for your clients or your students. But the beauty of it is you only really need to have to do it once. And once you've created this product online, you're then able to sell it over and over again to multiple people.

What I also love about creating online courses is that unlike creating a physical product, so a physical product, like let's say, this mug that I have over here, unlike creating a product like this, your overhead to create a digital product is really, really low. And to give you an idea of some things that you might have to pay for to get started is a membership platform, whether that's kajabi, Thinkific, or teachable.

This is the platform where you're going to host the course. Now obviously, depending on how extreme you want to take your course you can invest in equipment like a better microphone or a better webcam to create a really high quality experience, but a lot of that isn't 100% necessary. So keep in mind that the fees and the costs to create an online program is virtually pretty low. And in fact, even if you don't choose a platform like kajabi, Thinkific, or teachable, there are a lot of free platforms that will also allow you to host courses as well. And so unlike this product right here with the physical product, as an entrepreneur who sells physical products, you're going to need to pay for inventory costs, shipping costs, manufacturing costs for every unit that you need to produce. And that creates a lot of overhead. And therefore, for an e-commerce business, let's say that it sells physical products, you're going to have a lot less of a profit margin versus a digital product like courses or ebooks or anything like that your profit margins are going to be very high.

And to give you an idea of last year in 2019, my profit margins in my business was about 60%. And that is really big. That includes all the people that I hire, the platforms that I invest in in order to keep my business running, but my profit margins were about 60% versus an e commerce company, their profit margins might be 20% 30% 40%, maybe if they have really great profit margins. And that's the nature of the two different business models. And so when you have a digital course business or you create digital products, keep in mind that the startup fee is actually quite low. But I want to tell you right now, there are so many different courses that exist on the internet.

There are courses about manifestation of courses that teach you how to use a journal courses about parenting courses about how to walk your dog properly. There are so many different courses that exist and as a matter of fact, E-learning is an industry that is booming right now. And by 2025, it is expected to hit $325 billion and so this is a really great opportunity to tap into Especially if you already have something that you're really good at and that you're willing to teach others to be good at. as well. More and more as time goes on E learning is going to be massive. A lot of people prefer to learn online. And so again, if you are good at something whether that is being a great mom, being a great calligrapher, being a great dog walker, being a great stylist, you have the opportunity right at your fingertips to create a digital course that you can sell to your audience or to whoever sees value in your product.

Now, this has to be said because I think that creating a digital course product is great, but it is easier said than done. And I personally believe there are three things that would make it a little bit more successful and scalable if you decide to go this route. Now anyways, the three things that I believe would make a digital course product successful number one is you need to make sure you have a repeatable process that is designed to get results. So what this means is that this is a process that you don't have to customize for every person that goes through your program.

It's a process that whoever goes through it is going to get results if they put in the work and if they follow what you teach to the tee because that's also another topic that we can dive into. But basically, a course doesn't work unless you actually do the work right. But anyways, you need to have a repeatable process that is designed to get someone results. The second thing is you need to be very clear about who your course is for and that it's niched down. This is really important and it links back to the first tip that I just gave in order for a process to Have a high success rate of getting people results, you need to be super specific on who is the right fit for your course. So let's say for my digital course product, it's designed for new coaches who don't have pay clients yet to get their first few paid clients.

If I had told people that this course is for anyone and everyone, then my process that I have in my course, wouldn't work for everyone that goes through. And that's why it's really important that you are super specific about who your course is for. Let's say you're creating a course about dog walking, it's not going to work for someone who has a cat or who has a hamster. And so you need to make it crystal clear in your marketing and in your positioning that it is only for a specific type of person who has a dog. So be very, very clear on that.

And then the third thing that I believe will make a digital course product business scale a lot faster and get passive income a lot faster. traffic and visibility, you can absolutely sell digital courses with a very, very small audience and be successful at it. I know tons of people who have. But keep in mind that the lower priced your product is. So let's say it's a $10 course, imagine how many students you would need to enroll every single month in order to make a 10 k a month or have a six figure business you would need a lot. And so the more expensive your course is, the less traffic you might need in order to hit your income goals. But the cheaper your courses are the lower price ticket, your course is, you're going to need a lot more traffic. So these are the three things that you definitely want to keep in mind. But when you have these three things put together digital course products are a really great way to create passive income for yourself. And it really ranges from month to month. Let me give you an example of what we make in our business through selling digital courses. There are some months where we have six figure months.

There are other months where we make $50,000 and others Where we make a little bit more, it really ranges from month to month. But the beauty of it is, is that I have already put all of my work into this one product, and it's selling on autopilot as new students are enrolling into our program. Now obviously, the numbers that I just shared with you are my number and are very unique to my business and the way that I've set things up.

But for you, it could be something completely different. There are other course creators who are making way more than me, or there are some people who do it as a side hustle and get an extra $500 $2,000 $10,000, you know, $500 a month from selling digital products. Now, at this point, you might also be thinking to yourself, okay, I just broke down the three things that she believes makes a core successful. I don't have any of these three things. I don't have a repeatable process. I'm not sure if I can get people results. I don't know what the niche would even be. And I also not have a place where I even have an audience to sell to. So what do I do? Well, this leads me to the second income stream that I have that I think is really, really achievable. Even if you have a small audience and even if you aren't sure whether or not your process can get people results, and that is one on one coaching, or consulting and here's a fun fact before I became a course creator, before I packaged everything that I knew into my Academy, which is the program that I offer today, I used to do one on one coaching, slash Consulting and this is perfect for those of you who maybe aren't clear whether or not what you teach or what you coach on or what you offer can really work.

So instead of selling a course, that is one too many people, you instead work one to one with another person. And that way you're able to customize, you're able to truly talk to that person, one on one, understand what their needs are, get feedback, and also get to the level where you could potentially charge high ticket because remember, courses are generally a little bit less expensive versus one on work when you actually are dedicating a lot of time to build a program for someone, a lot of times actually hold someone's hand, coach them, consult them, whatever it is, you can command higher prices. And that's going to be a really great cash injection that you get into your business while also validating your process. And making sure that is repeatable for multiple people before you package it into a course working with private clients at the one on one level is also great because you get the flexibility of working with a variety of people so that you can really fine tune your niche and figure out what exactly is your zone of genius who exactly is your ideal client and in fact, my program helps a lot of new coaches do this. And a lot of my students actually one day want to be course creators, which is awesome. But first, they need to have an offer.

First, they need to know their niche. They need to know exactly what they can offer and learn how to sell that offer. And so Even in my program with our students who are working with one one clients, right now, we've had students make four figure months on top of working their corporate jobs.

This is amazing. And even when I started working at the one on one level, I used to work for free to test out. what I could do, what I couldn't do whether I could get people results, and then eventually I started charging, I started charging $500, then 1500 dollars, then $2,000, then 3000 4000 5000, to the point where month to month I was making a $10,000 month from working with people one on one. And then once I realized, whoa, this is my zone of genius. I'm good at what I do, I can get people results at the one on one level. It's now time to create a course and then I packaged everything that I was teaching, plus everything new that I've learned into a course. And now today I have the academy.

So as you can see, even if you're someone who wants to create a course one day, you can add Absolutely do that. But first, validate your course idea, validate whether or not you can get people results at the one on one level first. And one last thing that I want to mention because we're talking about multiple income streams here, you can be a course creator and charge one on one services on the side.

So for me if I wanted to, I could announce to YouTube and I could announce on my Instagram and say, Hey, everyone, I'm opening up five spots for private coaching or private consulting, and boom, I would be able to make income that way on top of having a course that I sell on the side so you could have both and increase the different streams of income that you have. So again, To give you an idea of the money that I make through this income stream last year,we made $30,000 off of just one on one coaching services, and then eventually transitioned to passive income products, such as digital courses, which again, like I mentioned earlier on in this book represents about 80 to 90% of my monthly income, and is where all my energy is dedicated to now moving on to the third income stream that I have.

And this is an obvious one, and that is youtube adsense revenue. So by posting content online and being monetized on YouTube, every month, I get money from it. Now, obviously, you would need to make sure that you have your 1000 subscribers and your 1000 hours of watch time in order to get monetized. But the moment that you hit that mark, you're then able to make money passively through the adsense revenue that you get paid from by YouTube and to give you an idea of how much money we make on YouTube.

Every month, we make About three to $4,000. And last year in 2019, we made a total of $37,000 just from posting content on YouTube and just from adsense revenue alone, which is a completely passive income stream for my business and for myself and an awesome thing about YouTube is that once you post a video one time and you are monetized that video time and time again, will make you money.

However, it is really, really fulfilling and also what I find is that creators and influencers are on the rise. People don't want to consume content that is super commercialized and super polished. They prefer to consume content from people who remind them of themselves. And that's why YouTube is such a successful platform.

And as much as so many people hate on YouTube, and how YouTube doesn't pay its creators Well, well, to be honest, Instagram isn't really paying any creators, Facebook isn't really paying any creators. So YouTube really is an awesome platform if you want to create content and also get paid for it. Now, obviously, everyone's results on YouTube are going to be different. My pay on YouTube based on my adsense revenue is going to be different from another YouTuber who maybe has more subscribers than me is in a different niche or has more views or whatnot, it's just going to be different. So just keep that in mind as well. But what I also want to mention and this is a hot tip, because remember in the beginning of this book, I mentioned that I would make sure that every income stream that I mentioned, I'm going to give a hot tip on for YouTube if you are considering starting a channel something that you need to know is that for Every niche, you get paid differently.

And what I mean by this is yes, you could have a lot of subscribers, yes, you could have a lot of views. But what it really comes down to is the niche that you're in. And that's what's really gonna determine what your cost per thousand is. So

CPM is a metric that we track here on YouTube. And basically, this is the amount of money that an advertiser is willing to pay you for every 1000 views that you produce.

So for example, my channel I could have a $10 CPM, so $10 for every 1000 views that I generate, versus another channel who might have a different CPM that is potentially $50 or $100, which is massive, or maybe compared to another channel, their CPM might be $5 or $2. So depending on the niche, you're going to get paid differently and this is the tip that I have for you, especially if you are considering to be on YouTube, and you are using YouTube strategically because you want to make extra income, I'm going to share with you some niches that are generally going to have higher CPM. And the reason why these niches and these industries have higher CPM is because the advertisers in these industries have a bigger budget and are more willing to spend money on these industries alone.

So for example, real estate, finance, social media, anything tech related, beauty, gaming, these are all massive industries where there's a lot of lucrative opportunities for advertisers to spend money on and therefore your CPM, your cost per thousand is going to be a lot higher than other niches. So if you are considering starting a YouTube channel for strategic reasons, because you want to make some passive income with AdSense, then really keep that in mind for your channel niche.

Now, there are some industries that don't make as high of a CPM and that is anything related to pranks because there's not many advertisers that want to put their ads on prank videos and maybe Anything controversial or taboo. So these types of niches, you might want to reconsider, especially if your sole goal is to make money through Adsense revenue.

Now, obviously, if it's your passion to have a comedy account, and you want to do pranks on people, do that. But it is shown that educational content is a lot more profitable than entertaining content. So again, if you're considering being a YouTuber, and you want to make money through AdSense, just keep that in mind. Now, before I dive into the next income stream that I have, I do want to make sure that nobody is discouraged from starting a YouTube channel because of what I just said. I want to make sure that even if you are planning to start a channel that is more for entertainment purposes, and it's for, you know, putting pranks doing, you know, taboo jokes or doing anything related to politics that might be a little bit controversial. You absolutely can.

And in the next few income streams that I'm going to share, it's also going to be related to you starting a YouTube channel. Any social media platform that generates you traffic and how you can monetize aside from adsense revenue, right, so the next income stream off of that point is affiliate links.

Affiliate links is a really great way to make passive income, especially if you have an audience and if you have the traffic for it, and what affiliate links basically are, is if you really enjoy using a product or a service or a piece of software, get a code for it, or get a link to it and refer it and share it with your audience or anyone for that matter.

And if that person clicks on the link, and they make a purchase, then you're going to get commission from that. So that is what affiliate marketing basically is. And for me, I have links everywhere. I have links in my YouTube description. I have links on my website. I have affiliate links when I promote a product on my Instagram and I just so happened to have a link and for us how much money we make off of affiliates really varies month to month. But on average, we make about two to $4,000 passively every month, just through affiliates alone. And in fact, in February, I believe we had one of our bigger months, when it comes to affiliate marketing, we made $7,000 passively, just from affiliates in February.

And this is insane. And this is all for me just simply talking about products that I already enjoy using recommending software to people and working with brands that I really, really believe in and giving a code to someone if they want to join with no pressure intended. And so this is a really awesome way for many of you guys, if you guys do have social media platforms to capitalize on and to just make extra income off of promoting things that you already enjoy using anyways. Now here is my hot tip when it comes to affiliate and this is something that I've learned through the year and a half that.

I have been an affiliate for Amazon or for something Where products or for other companies and all these different things. And what I've learned is, when you are starting out, even if you aren't interested in affiliate marketing yet, let's say you are just starting your business or whatnot, really be strategic with the platforms and the services that you use. And what I mean by this is, if I were to go back in time, I really wish that I considered a company's affiliate program as one of my decision drivers of whether or not I want to use their product or not. So for example, let's say email marketing software. This is just a random example. You know, instead of just buying or investing or paying for an email marketing software every single month and only looking at the features, I wish that I took that extra step to understand their affiliate program? What is the payout for that affiliate program in order to determine my decision of whether or not I want to use that service or product or software.

The reason why I'm mentioning this as a tip is because oftentimes, we don't know whether or not we'll be an affiliate one day, you might be using a software like ConvertKit, or Active Campaign or drip or MailChimp. And you might really love it for your business. And you might really want to recommend it to other people.

But if they don't have an affiliate program, that kind of stinks, or if they do have an affiliate program, but their payout is negligible, or maybe they don't have a good payout for their influencers, then that also stinks. And so I would have really wished that I considered the affiliate side of things as I was choosing which products and services to use for my own business.

Now, that's tip number one. Another tip when it comes to affiliate marketing is track it. Okay, so for a very long time, I was just promoting things left, right, front and center. You know, I was just doing affiliate links for things not really thinking too much of it because I didn't really think that I would make that much money off of affiliates. It wasn't until a couple months ago when I told my team Hey, I'm actually wanting to track this now like, let's actually compile all the money that we've made from affiliates and put it in a spreadsheet for us to understand which affiliates are the best performing for us.

And based on what is best performing and what is actually making us the most income, we will make more of an effort to push that to our audience. Why? Because our audience is clearly enjoying the services a lot more than these other ones. And that way, I'm able to actually focus my efforts in the products and services that benefit both me and my audience as well.

It doesn't make sense to continue promoting something that nobody is interested in. Right. And that's why it's so important if you are thinking of being an affiliate for any product or service, that you're actually tracking the performance of these affiliates so that you can really be strategic with where you put your efforts towards now.

These two hot tips that I'm sharing with you, it's going to help you increase your payouts a lot more. And it's also going to make sure that you are a lot more confident and a lot more willing to promote these products. So remember, the first tip that I mentioned, is to make sure that when you're starting out and you're choosing products and services that you consider their affiliate program because in order for you to be in integrity as an influencer, as an entrepreneur, as a content creator, you want to be promoting products that you love that you use yourself and that you can speak to.

But if that program or that service isn't necessarily compensating you for talking so highly about them, then there's a little bit of a disconnect, and you're not going to be as excited to talk about something that you already enjoy using. So that is why I mentioned tip number one, if you want to be in a business of integrity and promote products that you really love, then reverse engineer the process.

And make sure that the products that you are using in your business right now that they already have really great affiliate programs so that you'll be more than happy to continue using that service and get paid to recommend it at the same time. The second thing about tracking your data, this is also really important because you as the influencer as the content creator, as the entrepreneur, you are going to personally feel a lot more invested and a lot more excited to talk about someone else's products or services or software, knowing that your audience loves it as well.

And again, you get compensated as the reward of recommending these amazing programs, software's products and services to your audience. So just want to mention why I mentioned those two Hot Tips for you because I think that a lot of people, they don't spend enough time tracking things and they don't think about affiliate marketing as strategically as they should be in order to increase their confidence in the product and increase their payout potential that you can have from recommending products that you already love.

Now moving on to the fifth income stream that I'm To make online and that is brand deals, this is different from affiliate links. So affiliate links is me linking something, and then making a commission off of that link. Whereas brand deals is when a brand will pay me a lump sum in order to talk about their products in a video or in an Instagram story. Now, for me, in my business, I don't make a lot of money through brand deals, to be honest.

And that's because I don't really need to do brand deals in order to make a living for myself. And I also find that a lot of brands that reach out to me I have never used their products before and very similar to what I said earlier on is that you want to run a business of integrity and you don't want to promote products that you don't use yourself. Or at least that's my philosophy. So I actually turned down a lot of brand deals and that's allowed me to really build a very strong trust between you guys.

If you know that I'm promoting a brand, then you know that it's something that I actually use because I'm not that type of person. That is always going to rely on brand deals in order to put a roof over my head and food in my belly. And so for me, it's not consistent income when we have brand deals. But when we do have brand deals, we make about two to $3,000 every single time, depending on the package.

Now again, here's my hot tip for you, when it comes to brand deals, you want to make sure that you are very data driven when you approach brands or when brands approach you. So for example, I'm going to give you what my media kit looks like. It's very data driven. I tell brands, what is the percentage of females and males in my audience? all these important stats for these companies to determine whether or not they want to invest in me as an influencer, because again, they don't really care about me.

They care about the audience that I bring, and so the more data that I can get. Give them about my audience, the better. Now only this, I also give them a lot of data on my channel performance, my Instagram performance and everything like that. A lot of brands and companies want to make sure that they're going to get a good return on investment. And they also want to make sure they're not investing in influencers that have bought their subscribers or bought their followers. And so for me, I always include my Social Blade stats, I include my watch time, I include my impressions, my reach all the different types of data points that a brand would care about, in order for them to forecast the ROI. Not only this, I also share with them other leverage that I have. So I'm not just only sharing my YouTube channel, but I'm also sharing the fact that I have an email list of 60,000 people. These are my open rates.

I have a Facebook group, I have an Instagram, I have a podcast in order for me to create that mass leverage to show to the brand. And another hot tip that I have for you is that brands again, like I mentioned, want to make sure that there's an ROI So anytime that you can include data that shows past performance, it's going to be really, really great. So for example, for me, in order for a brand to really understand what I can bring to the table, I'll maybe show them screenshots of my performance with my other affiliates.

And I'll say, Hey, you know, this is my average click through rate with my Amazon affiliates. This is how much money and income that I've produced for Amazon based off of the affiliate links that I share with my audience. This is another example of me working with a brand and how much revenue we generated or how many clicks we generated. And that's going to allow that brand who's considering me as an influencer, that they want to work with, it's gonna really help them make that judgment call of whether or not I am worth the investment. So that is a hot tip that I have for you when it comes to dealing with brands. Now onto the last income stream that I have. And that is stocks. So actually, the moment that , we are in the midst of the pandemic. And not only this, since starting my business, I have completely neglected my stock portfolio. And so when I actually logged in to check actually forgot the password and my username, but when I logged into check, I realized that I'm actually losing money off of my portfolio.

So I have lost $2,000 off of it. And so with stocks it is you know, something that goes up and down and you never know how the market is going to react. So right now the market is down, which by the way is a good thing because that means that a lot of stocks are on discount and it's the perfect time to invest in stocks right now as we speak, especially since a lot of the prices have really really gone down.

So if you are interested in investing now is really the perfect time because literally every company is on a discount. But anyways, I started investing in index funds. And I started to do a little bit of stock picking, I don't do too much of it. And there was a time where I also invested in crypto currencies, I lost a lot of money in crypto currencies. But there was a time where I was investing a lot in this area. And this is another income stream that I have, even though right now, it's not making me any money. But this is something to consider for you, especially during this time when the market is down. So remember, the rule of thumb is you want to buy low, so you want to buy stocks and buy index funds and buy whatever when the prices are low, and then you want to sell high, meaning that when the prices go up, you want to sell that stock so that you can make a return on it. Now, as I mentioned, the first two things that I got started with were index funds, and what index funds are is that instead of buying specific companies, so for example, you buy a couple stocks in Apple, and you buy a couple stocks in Tesla, when you invest in index funds, you are essentially investing in an entire index.

So let's say instead of investing in specific companies, I'm now investing in the entire s&p 500, which means that I have now bought a little bit of every single company that is within the top 500 companies in the US within the s&p 500 index that is an index fund. So if the s&p 500 goes up, my portfolio will go up as well. If the s&p 500 is down like it is right now, then my portfolio will go down as well. And this is how you can really diversify your risk a little bit more. Now, obviously, with stock picking.

And that means you only buy an apple or you specifically only buy in Tesla, or you specifically buy an Amazon and you create your own little portfolio of different stocks that you've bought in multiple companies, you have a potential of higher returns. So if only those companies thrive and all the other companies fail, then you're gonna make a huge return out of it, but it's a lot riskier. So if those companies fail, then you'll also fail as well. And so that's the difference between stock picking, which is a little bit more riskier. versus investing in something safer such as index funds. For me, I rationalized it as Okay, well, I personally think the s&p 500. From a long term perspective, it's always going to go up, I believe that the market will always go up. You know, obviously, there's going to be months or years where it goes down, but as a whole within maybe a 20 to 50 year span, I believe the trend is that it's going to go up. And so that's why I personally decided to invest in index funds first.

Now, obviously, there are some companies that I invest in that are just very specific, for example, Weed Stocks, or other different types of industries. But I personally believe that if you are getting started with investing, especially DIY investing, meaning that you are investing yourself, and you're not necessarily relying on a fund manager to help you do it, then I personally believe that investing in something like index funds is a really great way to start.

And to this day, I still have my portfolio, even though I don't really touch it. And I actually think as a matter of fact that I probably should look at it more and invest in it more. But I think that this is a really great way for you to create passive income for yourself in the long term. Now, again, by no means am I a fund manager. I am not a financial expert. I really barely know what I'm doing. But at least you have a starting place to understand the different things that are available to you in order to make more income by leveraging your online presence or just by taking action alone for a lot of these things. Especially let's say investing in stocks. It might take a little bit of research but It's very, very easy to get into if I can figure it out, you can figure it out.

So definitely put that ownership and self responsibility onto yourself to learn about income, how you can diversify how you can increase your income streams because it's really nice to not only rely on one income stream in order to put a roof over your head or to put food in your belly. But anyways guys, I hope that you enjoyed, I hope that you found it informative. And I hope that you learn something new in at least one of these income streams that I have presented.